Acme Attractions
Jeannette Lee & Don Letts

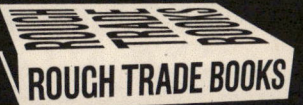

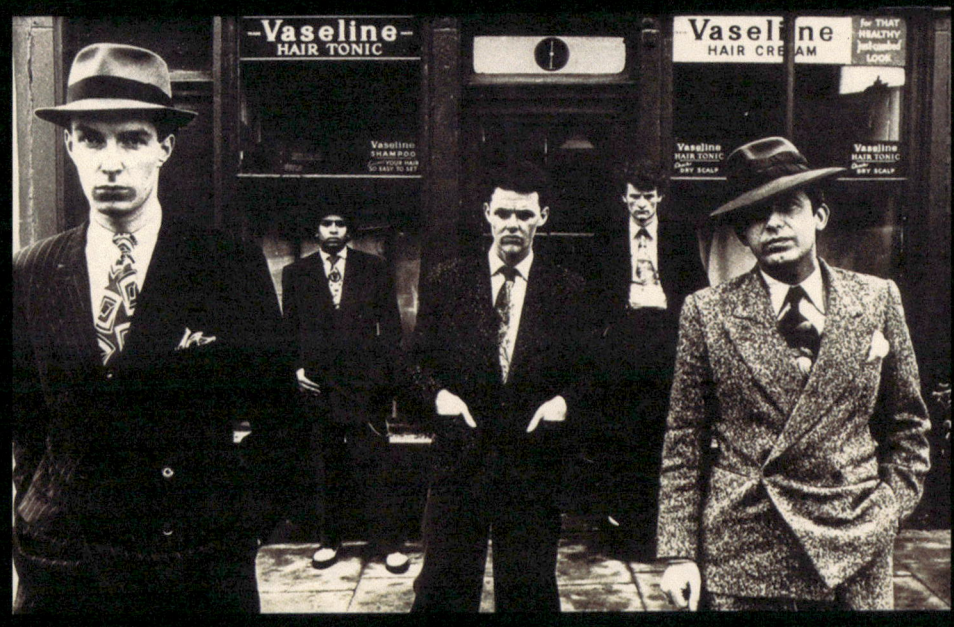

ACME ATTRACTIONS
Jeannette Lee & Don Letts

These funny, tender, clear-eyed and frank reminiscences on the history of what might appear at first glance to have been merely a clothes shop on the Kings Road in the mid-to-late 70s, in fact present the reader with a concentrated dose of the cultural, political and social movements that shaped the culture of the whole country in the following years.

Acme Attractions saw both the dog-days of glam and the vital embryonic period of punk, and Don Letts' and Jeannette Lee's conversation about their memories of the place serve as testimony not just to the period, but also to the bravery and commitment of youth, the enduring effect of our first forays into adulthood through love, self-expression and art. The specific texture of London at the time becomes delicately drawn through two people's very human experience and we find ourselves immersed in the seismic shifts of culture and politics that continue to define that period in the city's history, with revolutions in music, race relations, sexuality and fashion, but told with the warmth and acute observation that can only come through the kind of direct contact Letts and Lee are able to impart. It's a story about how sometimes you are lucky enough to be around right when things are being made, but how in the middle of all that history, people are still muddling along, falling in and out of love, making rash decisions, suffering the smaller, personal tragedies that make humans rather than epochs—being young, in other words.

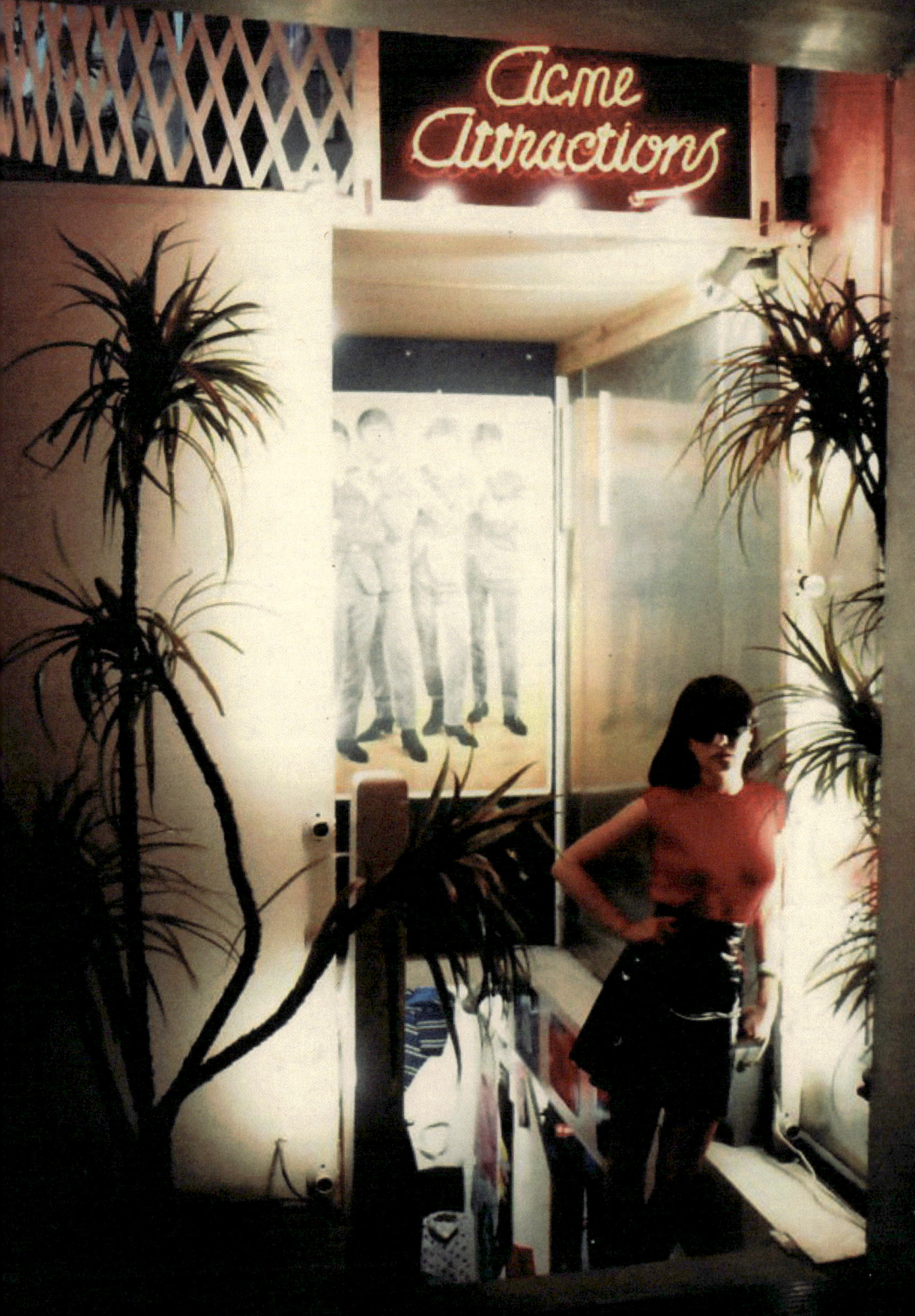

DON LETTS It's a funny old story Acme Attractions. In Brixton, this funky little shop opened that I never understood. It was dark and dingy and it sold jukeboxes, pinball machines and one-arm bandits—totally incongruous—nobody in Brixton was going to be buying any of that shit but out of curiosity I walked in. It turned out it was run by this gentleman called John Krivine who I became friendly with. He was a really interesting character and this place was like—it's hard to explain—it was like the back lot of an amusement arcade so visually, really interesting. Anyway, I became friends with John and over the next few months he lets me know he has ideas of opening a shop on the Kings Road, Chelsea. He could see I was into fashion and he was going to open a stall in the Antiquarius, which was like a fuddy-duddy old antiques market in every sense of the word—people with big moustaches, checked jackets with leather elbow patches, yer know, old school. He set up this little stall that had a motorbike in there and some demob suits and a jukebox with my beloved reggae soundtrack which used to drive all the older people fucking nuts. It was a total culture-clash and they wanted me to leave. The basement of this place became available so we moved down there. That version of the shop was the one that got famous but the stall upstairs was important because it was the gateway to the basement. This is around the time I met Jeannette Lee and in those days it was all about soul music. We met at one of these soul clubs—I can't remember which one—I think it was the Lyceum or it could've been one of these chains that were around called Bird's Nest. We were all doing this kind of soul circuit back then.

JEANNETTE LEE *I used to go dancing at the Lyceum on a Monday night—you'd go to different clubs on different nights back then but this particular night this irritating guy came up to me. I was sitting on the stage and he walked towards me with make-up on his eyes, earrings in his ears, wearing a plastic packa-mac and winklepickers. It was 1975. He comes walking towards me and he said, erm excuse me do you mind if I sit here 'cos my feet are killing me and I need to change my shoes. I thought how rude and then shortly afterwards someone told me that this was the infamous Don that I'd heard about. He was infamous—we won't mention names but at the time I was hanging out with some kids and let's just say you knew their sister. I was desperately trying to give him a wide berth but he kept talking to me. I really liked his plastic granny mac and eventually I cracked and asked where he got it and he told me he*

© Sheila Rock

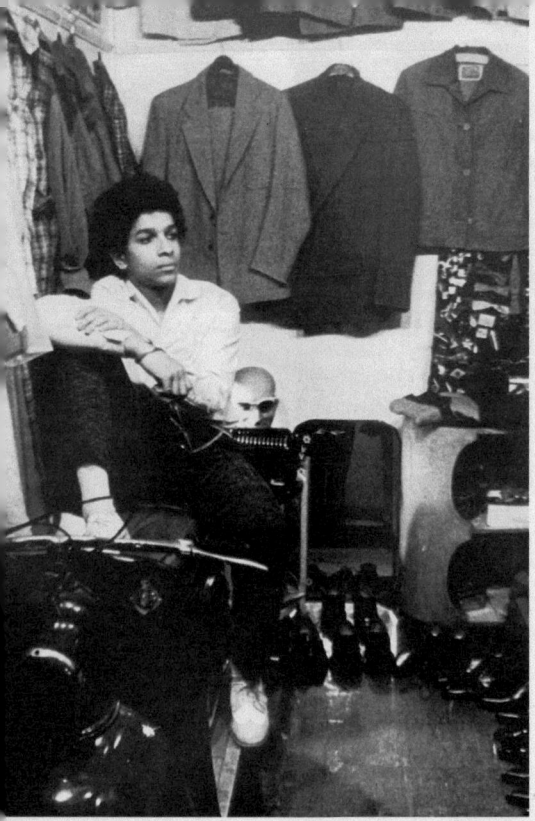

plastic mac, then I went home and had to convince my mum that I was going to drop out of education.

I got you to drop out of education? I did that?

No I did it...

I offered you a job so I did it. I don't remember that though, I just remember we were all out of education.

Almost every degenerate thing that's ever happened to me in my life is something you've instigated.

The shop was casual, we'd be sitting around like we are now—it was a really relaxed vibe. We did all-sorts down there. We did drugs down there—don't know how much we want to talk about that—anything you could do at home or a club we did it in the shop, let's put it that way—and more! People would come and hang out for ages and they wouldn't hang out because of me—I'd be sitting there with my dark glasses apparently looking intimidating. They were hanging out to talk to Jeannette. She was good cop. It was good cop, bad cop.

I was just friendlier than you. It was like a social club. My involvement started in 1975, which was as soon as it went down into the basement and at that time there was lots of interesting things happening in

sold them and if I was to come to such and such a place he'd have one that would fit me.

I took a shine to her, I wouldn't be so presumptuous to say she took a shine to me, but I definitely took a shine to her.

There was no plastic mac when I got there which was very disappointing but he told me almost straight away that the stall was moving downstairs and asked if I might like to work there with him. What I found out later was that it wasn't even his place so he couldn't offer me this job anyway. So that's what happened, he asked me to work there with him. I got a trench coat instead of a fashion and in music. The owners Steph Raynor and John Krivine—particularly Steph—would drive around the country and find old warehouses full of stock that hadn't sold in the 50s and 60s.

Even stuff from the 40s too that they would find in warehouses in Liverpool. Wemblex shirts, remember them?

Yeah of course those shirts with the pin across the front? The winged sunglasses, plastic sandals, mohair sweaters, jellies.

When they realised this stock was running out they started to design and create stuff—either replicas or items they half-inched from Vivienne Westwood and Malcolm McLaren because we shared a tailor.

Vic was his name. He was once tailor to Vivienne and Malcolm and then when they started making more 'SEX' items rather than 'Let It Rock' he started making peg trousers and things like that for us and because of that we ended up being banned from SEX (the shop)—it started a rivalry between us that didn't exist before.

By this time, Acme's built up—it was a club man—it was packed. People would come there to find out what was happening in town, not just to buy clothes—clothes almost became secondary I think. We still sold

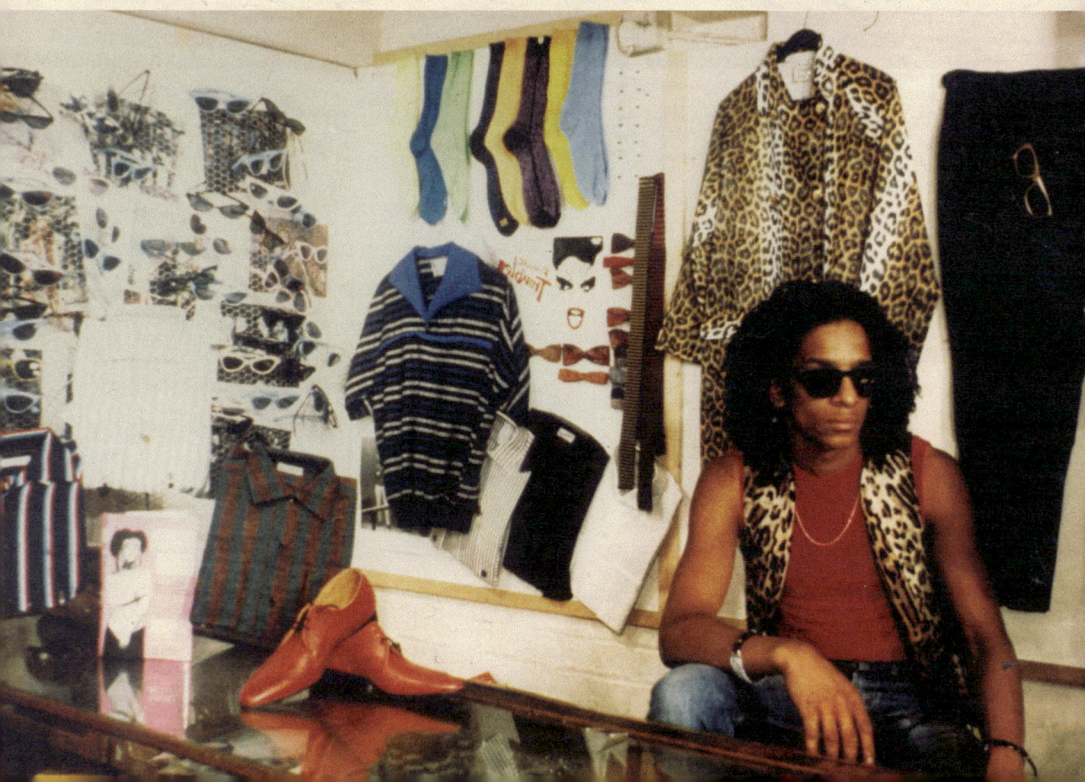

© Sheila Rock

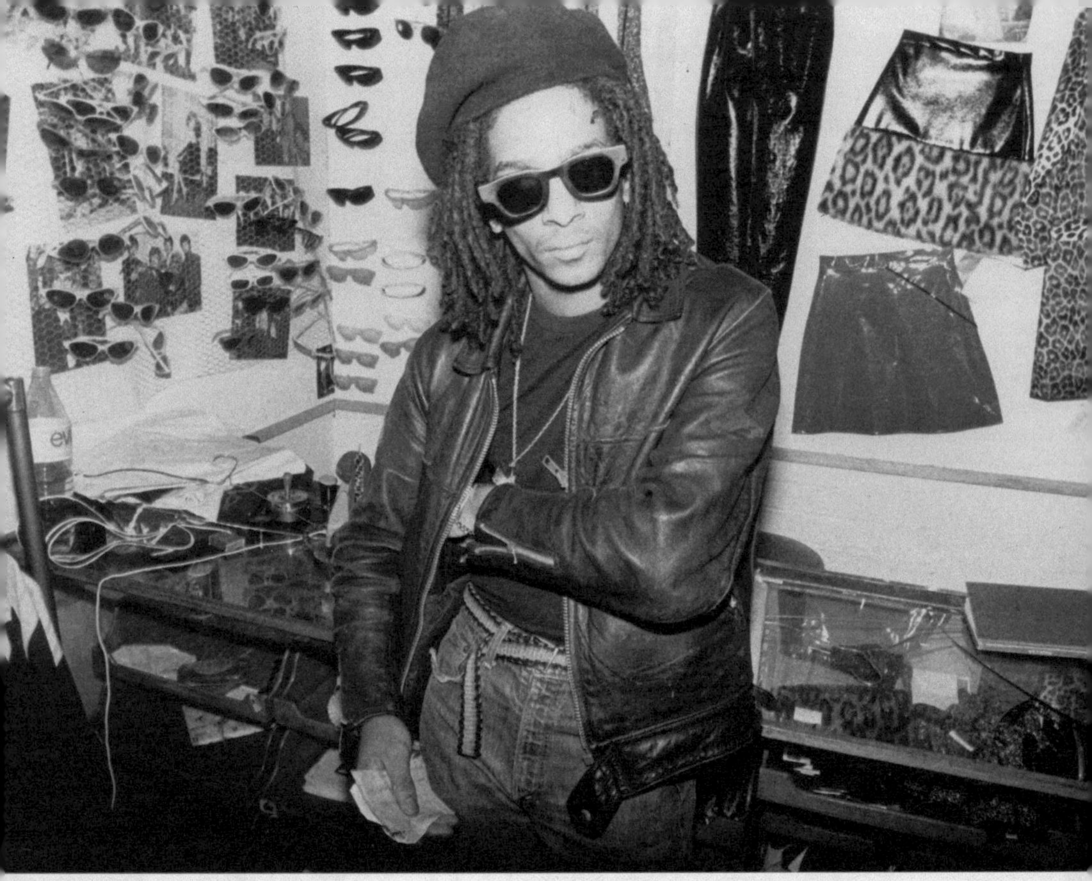

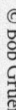

shitloads—my pockets were the till and her pockets were the till.

No, only yours!

Dresses and mini-skirts were hard to put cash in but our pockets were the till and it was more user friendly than Vivienne and Malcolm's shop. Their shop was definitely intimidating—there was no kind of, 'can I help you?' not that we did that but it was expensive too. Acme was more affordable. Peg trousers were £20. In Vivienne and Malcolm's shop they were £60 and their stuff was a bit more Eurocentric.

People would go between the two shops to be fair but they felt able to stay when they came to ours and they might've been a bit more intimidated down the road.

They'd go see Vivienne and Malcolm's stuff that they couldn't afford most of the time and if they couldn't steal it they'd be back down hanging out at ours.

All of the clothes we wore were from Acme Attractions and SEX.

© Bob Gruen

I used to know the guy there, Michael, and he always used to give me and Jeannette clothes to wear. The difference between the clothes that we sold and Viv and Malcolm's, is their clothes were really art. We couldn't claim that and have to give them massive props for that. Acme reflected the more multi-cultural way that England was heading and we had the reggae soundtrack—which was really important because you'd hear that before you had any idea of where the shop was and we still pissed off the people upstairs. People would ask where Acme was and they'd be told to follow the bass. You'd walk along the Kings Road and there's the Antiquarius—an old-fashioned kinda place—you walk through the doorway and pass a few stalls selling pipes for instance—you walk down some stairs and you literally enter this alternate world—totally separate from what was going on upstairs. You could hear it before you saw it. All these different tribes that were around at that time—they would all congregate at Acme.

It must've been quite intimidating to go down into the basement. It was brightly lit, with neon lights and pinball machines. It wasn't dingy at all, there were no windows in the basement but it was bright.

The only smell down there was weed.

Martin Brading, who's now a photographer, worked with us every Saturday. We had a few people who'd come in and help out. It was separate from the market upstairs—I don't think it was only full of fuddy-duddies, there was some interesting people up there. Michael and Gerlinde for instance.

Yeah, also Bernie Rhodes, who went on to manage the Clash, had a stall in there too and that was the only other one that was vaguely interesting—selling 45s and screen-printed shirts. He sold those in Vivienne and Malcolm's shop too as he was friends with them but it was a bit more contemporary and a bit more of an Acme vibe.

The other thing that was going on simultaneously was Andrew Logan's Alternative Miss World—so we had a crossover with all of that crew and they would come over and hang out in the shop.

Before punk, the big things on the Kings Road were the likes of Michael and Gerlinde, Andrew Logan, *Rocky Horror Picture Show*—that was the old crowd and they were kinda on the way out. A lot of it revolved around this shop called Jean Machine. Believe it or not, that was a trendy, hip place back then where all the freaks would be, but their time had passed with all the glam and Bowie thing and punk was just about to happen.

We had a couple of years from '75. Punk started happening late '76 so we had a year and a bit, which felt like 5 years because we were young, where the shop was full of peacocks. Everyone was watching John Waters' films and lots of men would come by in beautiful clothes dressed like women. It was a really creative hangout place for glamorous misfits and outsiders.

One of our early customers was John Beverley who went on to become Sid Vicious—he used to come round and see her all the fucking time. He was a pain in the arse—couldn't get rid of him. Stealing Jeannette's attention.

You were so horrible to him.

Yeah because he was stealing your attention—of course I'm gonna be pissed off. Anyone who took her attention for a long time—I didn't like that. The other thing is loads of other interesting people came in too like Peter O'Toole—remember him? He came in and he used to buy weed from me behind the counter. Bob Marley used to come in the shop when he lived on Oakley Street, which was around the corner. He would come down the shop and if I wasn't there he would try and pull Jeannette.

Here we go again. I can tell you one thing, which you'll be surprised by—I have never smoked dope in my life—not even once. I've done loads of other things. I think it's funny that I spent so many years with you and never smoked—it was such a big part of our lives.

Funny thing about Bob—by this time punk's happening—it's 1977 and he's round the corner and one day I went to get some money from him that he owed me and I'm wearing bondage trousers and I walked in and he said, Don Letts you look like one of those nasty punk-rockers. And I said, what are you talking about? I was young then and this is the mighty Bob Marley and I said, hold on a minute Bob these are my friends that you're talking about—they're not crazy baldheads, there's something going on, they're like-minded rebels. He basically told me to get the fuck out and he thought it was nonsense. He'd been reading the tabloids and he was getting very negative ideas about it. Three months later, a somewhat more informed Bob Marley wrote 'Punky Reggae Party'.

But anyway, there were a lot of drugs around—at least on the Kings Road—there were a lot of fucking drugs

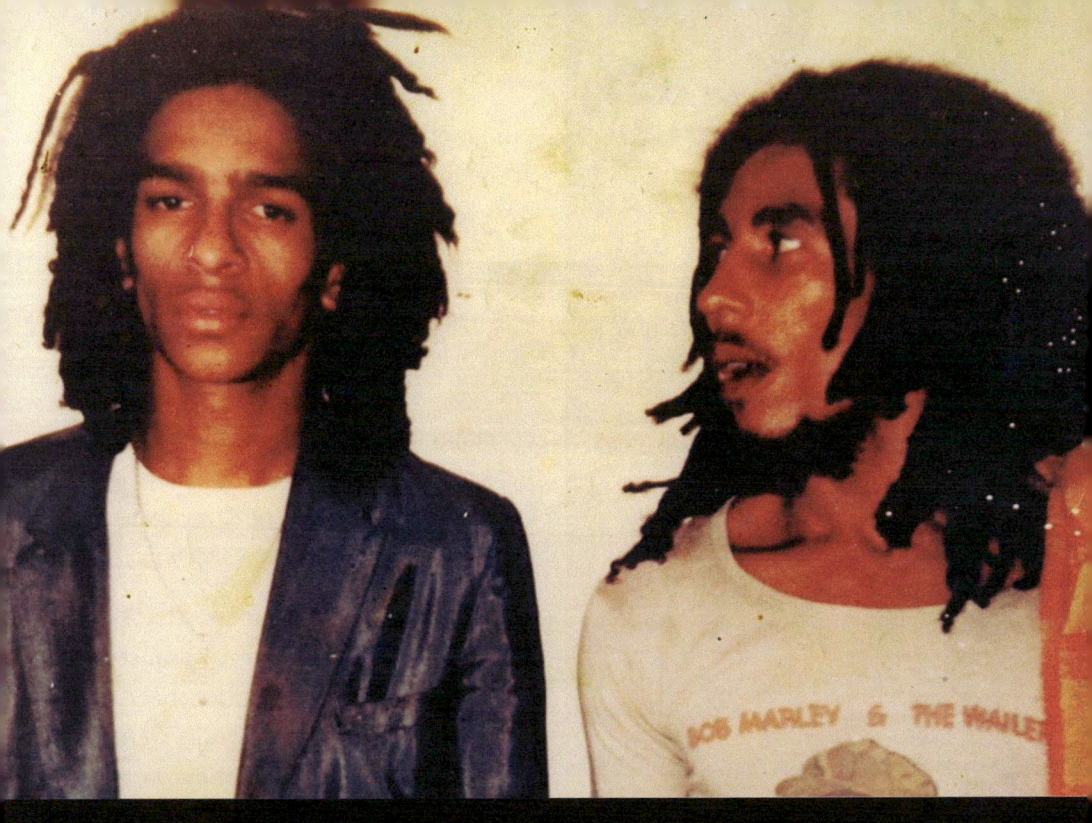

'I SAID, HOLD ON A MINUTE BOB THESE ARE MY FRIENDS THAT YOU'RE TALKING ABOUT—THEY'RE NOT CRAZY BALDHEADS, THERE'S SOMETHING GOING ON, THEY'RE LIKE-MINDED REBELS. HE BASICALLY TOLD ME TO GET THE FUCK OUT'

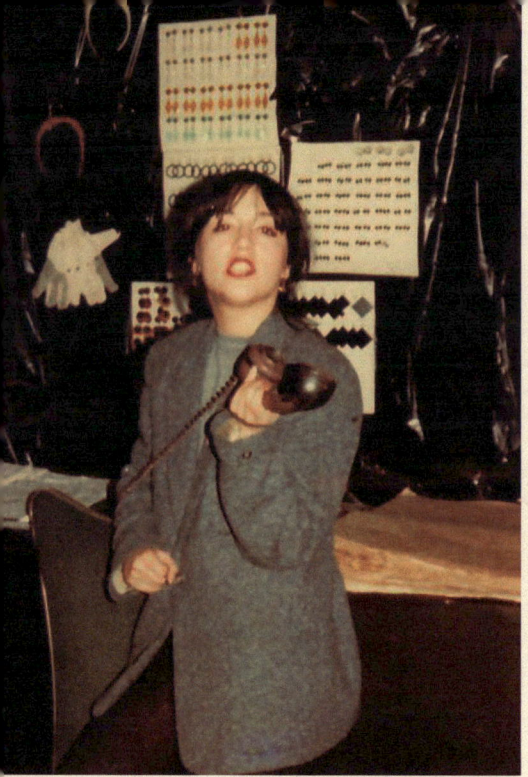

around and there was a healthy black market—let's put it that way man. I remember taking acid in the basement a few times—you took it as well.

The first time I took acid you gave it to me in the shop and then I remember John Krivine phoned up to say he was coming over. He didn't come over very often and you had to get rid of me because I was tripping. Someone came and picked me up and took me away.

Thinking about it—people had to do that a lot with you.

Get out of it—that's the only time I remember.

I did it once when I was DJing at the Roxy when I had a cyst on my eye. Remember that?

When the band went on at the Roxy, Don would have an hour off from DJing and that night he just disappeared. I couldn't find him anywhere. He had a cyst on his eye on this particular night, and it was freaking him out. Turns out he went to the eye hospital and they operated on him and they took it out whilst he was tripping.

I don't want to make out like that's all it was back then—but it was just part of the mix—I remember speed being a big deal then, downers were a big deal back then, somehow we became a conduit for it. People would come down there and kinda meet other people.

People would come in and offer stolen goods, they would come in with Cartier watches to sell because it was a place that attracted a funny mixture of rude boys and fashion people. Rude boys weren't interested in the clothes we sold, just the music, so it was a really weird mixture. At any point you might've seen a transvestite in one corner and a rude boy smoking a spliff in the other corner trying to sell you something that was nicked.

The cast of characters man, you could fill a book with just that.

Rudolf Nureyev came in wearing a cape, Patti Smith was someone we got friendly with down in the basement. Jordan used to hang out there a lot before she started to work for Vivienne and Malcolm. She was so far ahead of her time. She looked punk in 1974/5. She'd come up from Brighton in rubber skirts and fishnet stockings and bouffant hair—she was a trip.

She was an absolute original.

Straight out of *Pink Flamingos* or something. She was a really good friend for a while until Vivienne banned her from the shop. Once the rivalry started you couldn't let Vivienne know that you went to both shops. Billy Idol used to hang out at the shop—unfortunately.

To show you how extreme the mixture of people who would come in, we would have Patti Smith one day and then Daryl Hall in the other. People would hear about it. It was a place to be seen. Chrissie Hynde was part of the gang and there was a period where Chrissie had absolutely no money. She was trying to form a band and sometimes we would give her money to buy food. She's a good artist and started drawing on T-shirts for us, which we would then sell in the shop. I remember her not being very keen on Patti Smith and we kept asking her to do Patti Smith ones because we could sell them quite easily plus she was always in the shop.

Judy Nylon and Patti Palladin were down there a lot. When punk did explode—Acme was buzzing long before that, so it was already a scene—but when punk exploded you started seeing more of these dishevelled spiky-haired people hanging about in the shop and they turned out to be Lydon, Strummer, Siouxsie, and the Slits—we became friends with all of these people from Acme before the Roxy opened. Anyone who was anybody in the punk-rock scene passed through Acme.

One of the important things about Acme was, we would go home to Forest Hill and Don would make up these cassettes that we would play in the shop all the time.

The predominant sound in the shop was reggae but obviously we'd both get fed up of that occasionally and so we'd play some odd things— I remember what I used to love playing down there was Todd Rundgren's *A Wizard, a True Star*. No one listens to reggae 24/7, we're not that stupid but that was the soundtrack that worked best in the shop but yeah, we'd play other bits and pieces in there. We'd have a cassette player—the jukebox was mainly decoration, it was a Wurlitzer that played 78s. Big gaudy things with buttons on the side so it wasn't practical to use and it was there to advertise that we sold jukeboxes on the side, but we had them stored in a factory and sold them to rock stars like Jimmy Page for instance.

Quite early on, we became good friends with someone called Peter Dougherty who was an American exchange student from New York and he would stay with us and he was into American punk and would bootleg (for himself) every single show he went to so we got into the thing quite early on, before English punk really. Peter started this exchange—Don would make him reggae tapes and he would send us Television, Patti Smith, Richard Hell, Voidoids, Suicide—he would go to every gig, he was a bit obsessive and he would send us tapes of all these New York bands that no one else had access to. Mixed in with all the reggae we would be playing all this New York punk that no one had heard—it wasn't like now—there was no internet so there was no other way of hearing it.

We owe Peter big time—he went on to become a big shot in MTV and helped create *Yo MTV Raps*.

In later life, he'd carried on sending us bootleg tapes of bands like the Pop Group until he died about five years ago.

'ALL OF A SUDDEN YOU BEGAN TO SEE MOHAWKS AND SAFETY PINS AND THEN THE PAPERS STARTED SAYING, THIS IS WHAT PUNK'S ABOUT AND IT GOT A BIT CARTOONY VERY

The mixtapes though were quite a big deal because we used to sell them. The Pistols and the Clash would take them on their tour buses. Patti Smith and her lot would take them, Deborah Harry too.

It became a bit of a currency didn't it? The white punks were into reggae but didn't really know where to get it so they would come to Acme and Don and our crew capitalised on that as we'd sell them spliffs too—as they didn't know how to roll spliffs either—so they'd have ready-made spliffs and reggae that they couldn't access because they didn't know the places to get it.

We're underplaying the fashion thing though. In Robert Elms' book, *The Way We Wore*, a lot of people really liked Acme clothes. It became a magnet for people who lived outside London that would come for the mohair sweaters, the peg trousers, the jellies, the Marlow crepe-sole shoes, so yeah we're underplaying the clothes but it did strike a chord with a lot of people who were into fashion—without a doubt. Timeless British classics for the most part.

We had a load of kids that used to come from Newquay. Surfers. They'd buy the peg trousers. Peg trousers are tailored, have pleats at the waist and the legs bowl out and then are tight at the bottom. We had them in beautiful 60s colours—bright pink, fluorescent green, electric blue.

To go back to the Roxy, it definitely had a connection to Acme. The guy that opened the Roxy was a guy called Andrew Czezowski, who was Acme's accountant. He saw the punk thing was happening but the bands had no real place to play so he decided to open the Roxy and because of the reaction he saw to the music I was playing in the shop (predominantly reggae) he asked me to DJ there and that's what I played. We'd work all day in the shop and then we went to the Roxy until midnight, go home and probably stayed up 'til late listening to records. How did we do that I wonder?

I don't know, because when you're young you don't need much sleep. I think it's that simple... and the drugs!

We didn't start early the next day.

Yeah we did, we started at 10am.

Get out of it, we started when we wanted to. I remember a couple of times John was pissed off because we weren't there.

Yeah because we were supposed to be there at 10am and a couple of times we didn't arrive. I think I partly learnt my work ethic from you—you're like mr-have-to-be-there-

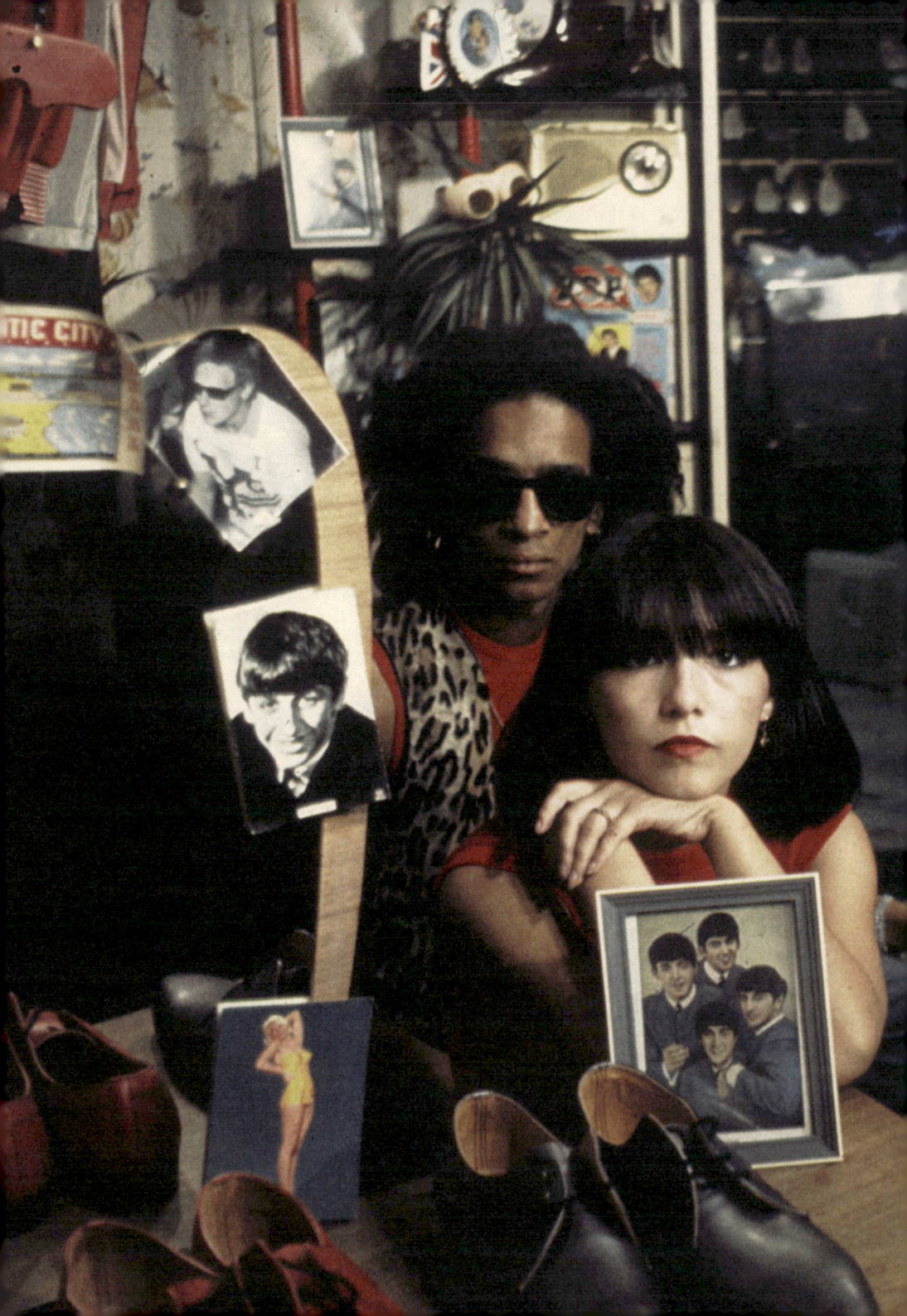

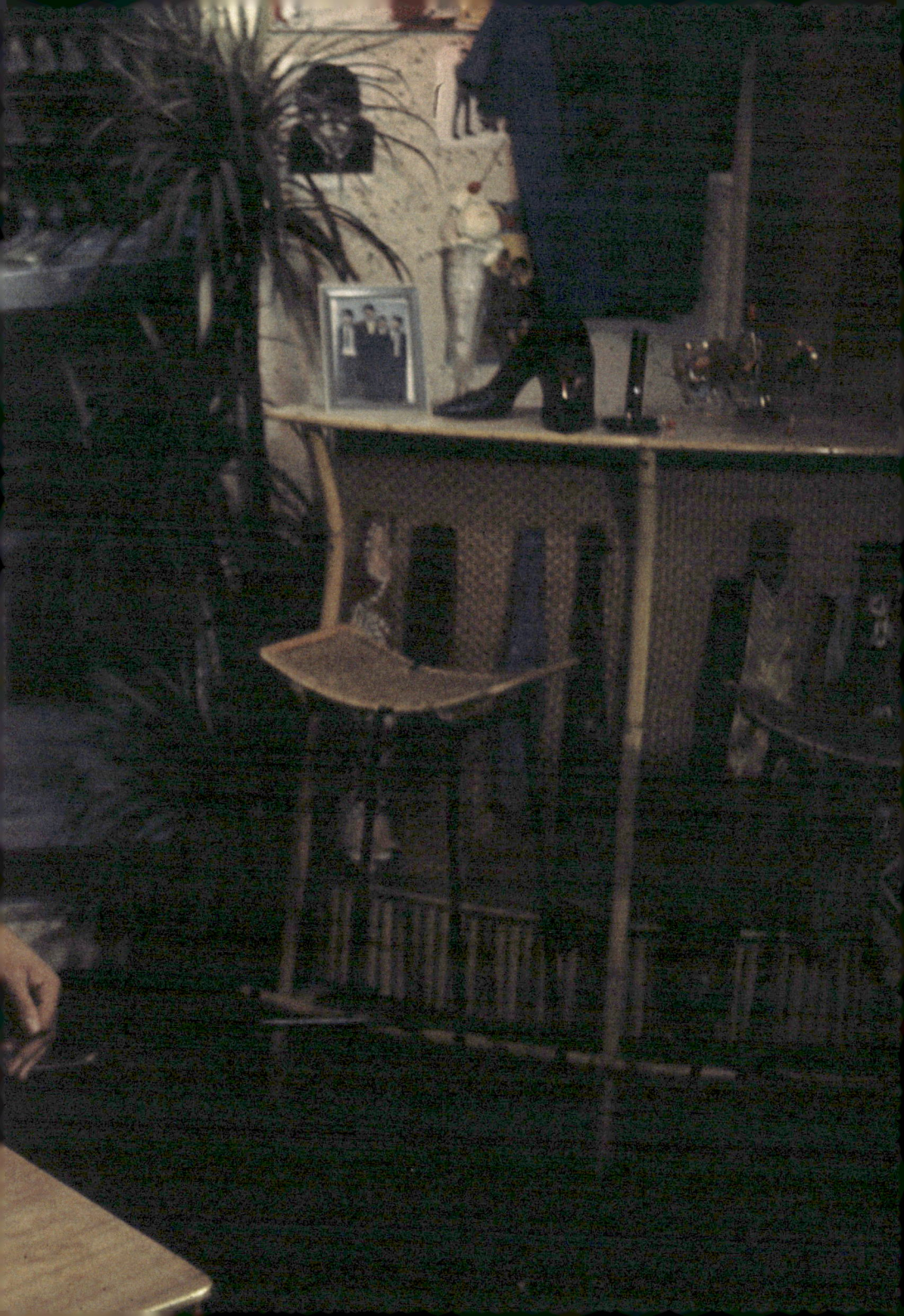

on-time so I do think we were there at 10am nearly every day.

You know the Patti Smith thing at the Odeon that we went to? People always go on about the 'punky reggae party' coming out of the Roxy in '77 and really it started in 1975. Basically Patti came into the shop, this is an Acme derivative story, because she's heard the reggae, and mentions she liked this guy called Tapper Zukie who happened to be a mate of mine and she said, Oh brilliant, bring him to the show. She invites me, Jeannette and Tapper to her sell-out show at the Hammersmith Odeon—we're standing in the wings of the stage, when she drags Tapper on and gives him a guitar—he can't play guitar. I'm killing myself with laughter when she drags me on stage and puts a mic in my hand. There's no such thing as air-mic so I break into the heaviest Jamaican slanguage I could muster chanting things like 'cramp and paralyse them' and 'those that worship Babylon'. All this time Jeannette is in the wings witnessing all this go down and I'd never been on the stage in my life but the point of the story is that this was the beginning of the punky reggae vibe because Patti was into reggae and that all really came through Acme, from her coming into the shop and getting friendly.

I remember her seeing the Cartier watch I'd acquired and pointing out she had one saying, two of a kind. I replied saying, I don't think so Patti!

And do you remember we went to Covent Garden where she played some impromptu thing. It was an after-show and she got up and Tapper sang with her and they sang 'Black Cinderella' or some shit. Anyway, a lot of things came out of Acme because a lot of people met there.

As we got nearer to punk, it would be a meeting place for people that wanted to be in bands and they would come in and talk to you about what band they were forming and who was in it and then you might have a suggestion of someone else who had been in the shop and was looking for a musician.

The Roxy officially opened on 1st January 1977 but actually I think it was open three weeks before that. They had a long soft-opening. It was the Clash that officially opened it. Besides all the Acme people that would be there, there was a whole load of people that picked up on the whole punk vibe. The Roxy was only open for three months, people don't realise that. 1st Jan 1977 and then three months later it was gone when the landlords tried to stage a coup, Andrew and all of us left and then they brought in a second lot of people which was almost second wave—UK Subs, The Exploited and all that stuff started to come when we weren't around. If I remember correctly, the Roxy opened just after that Bill Grundy thing with the Pistols, so we started to get some of the tabloid punk people in as well. All of a sudden you began to see mohawks and safety pins and then the papers started saying, this is what punk's about and it got a bit cartoony very quickly. Before that, everyone was individual I thought.

What was exciting for us was we were at the cusp of the changeover from kind of gay fashion/disco-dancing/glam—we were right at the crossover between glam and punk so in a space of a year we probably started off being glammy and ended up being as punk as you can imagine.

What a time! It's interesting how parallel our stories are. Working-class, white girl meets Black guy and they do all this shit.

Yes we've had a weird parallel existence. We've often done things at the same time throughout our life. I did film stuff with PIL, Don got his camera during the shop period, when we were going to the Roxy, one day he told me he was going to get a camera and that's how he made The Punk Rock Movie, filming at the Roxy as well as DJing.

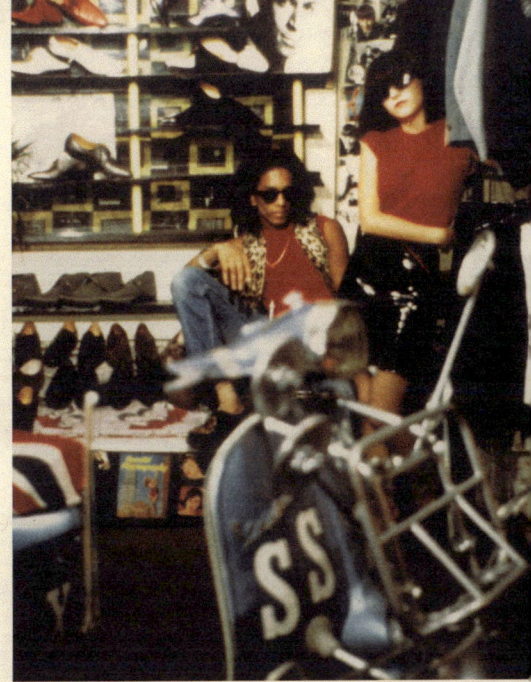

Never filmed in Acme. Probably one of the most stupid things I never did. Do you remember when we got busted with Bryan Ferret (our shop pet, a ferret)?

One of the things that was a really big part of our lives at the time was the SUS law (in England and Wales, the sus law (from 'suspected person') was a stop and search law that permitted a police officer to stop, search and potentially arrest people on suspicion of them being in breach of section 4 of the Vagrancy Act). The police were allowed to stop Black people and search them if they thought they looked a bit suspect so we would get stopped every other day. Don usually had some kind of flash car or something that drew attention to him and the police would stop us and he'd go into his routine spiel and speak to them

© Sheila Rock

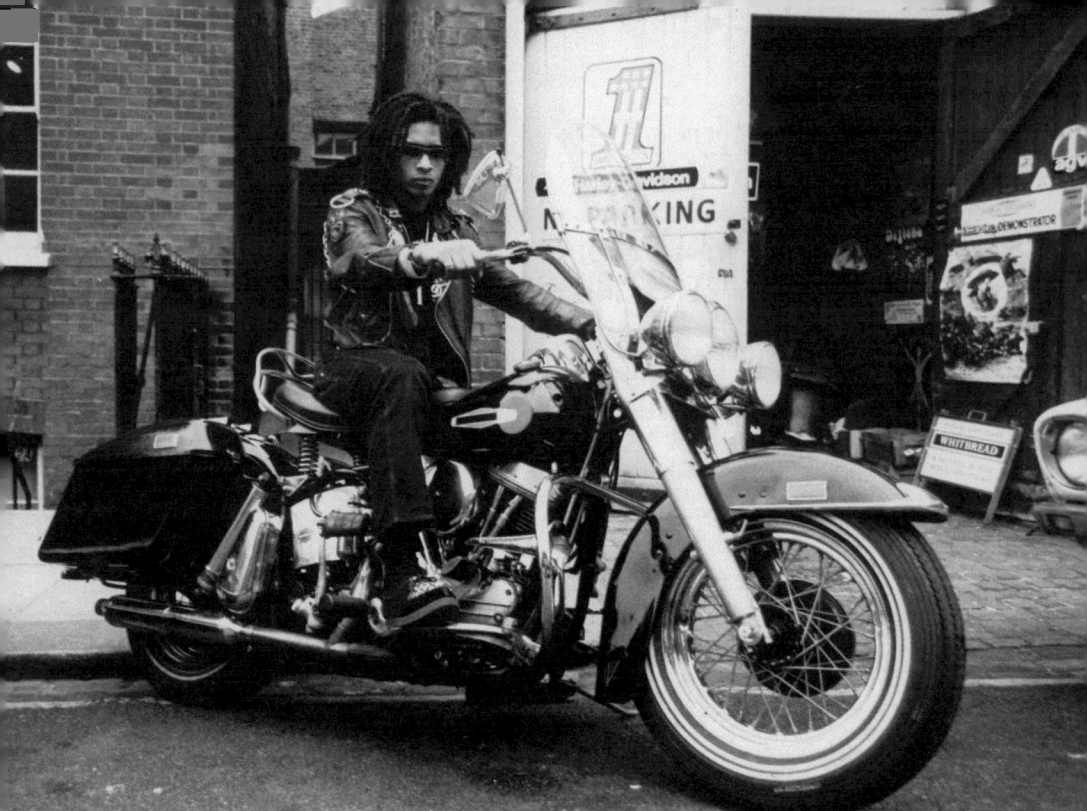

in the Queen's English which they weren't expecting—you know, Hello officer, what can I do for you officer, is there a problem?—and then he would put his arms in the air and cause a spectacle, which would distract them.

Whilst you'd run away with the drugs!

The police would get really embarrassed because he would draw so much attention. They hated you. They really had it in for you for a while after that. We weren't like drug smugglers or anything, it was always personal use.

Three Venezuelan gay guys, Gustavo, Gonzalo and Antonio became close friends of ours through hanging out in the shop—particularly with Jeannette. And Antonio the hairdresser was going to get chucked out of the country.

I was 17 at the time, and Antonio said he couldn't stay in the UK any longer and I think we said casually, that when I was 18 I would marry him. When I turned 18 he came back and asked if I was still up for it. I just couldn't bring myself to say no. I wasn't very happy about it but I really liked him so I did it. Sadly, six months later a truck driver hit him as he was running across the main road in Clapham. He was wearing a pair of pink peg trousers that *he'd bought from Acme. At the inquest the driver pretty much said the pink pegs were the only thing he noticed when he accidentally hit him. I was married and widowed at 18 years old...*

Those guys they were loud, proud and fierce. They weren't in the closet. They were beautiful people—absolutely beautiful. The gay community and the gay clubs were the best—probably still are!

All my favourite clothes came from SEX. Always. Or vintage—it wasn't called vintage back then it was called second-hand even if it was brand new as it would come from a warehouse. I definitely had a problem after the SEX shop stopped being SEX— I didn't feel like I could buy clothes in normal shops. For years, I just felt like nothing was interesting enough and I also felt some kind of really weird, devotional loyalty to Vivienne and the clothes that she used to make in that period. For ages I just wore black.

I didn't have favourite outfits as such, but it was the way we put stuff together. I remember someone saying to me that I was the first person he saw using rope as a belt—it was a kind of urban ragamuffin thing before ragamuffin came into the conversation. It was a mixture of Jamaican rude boy

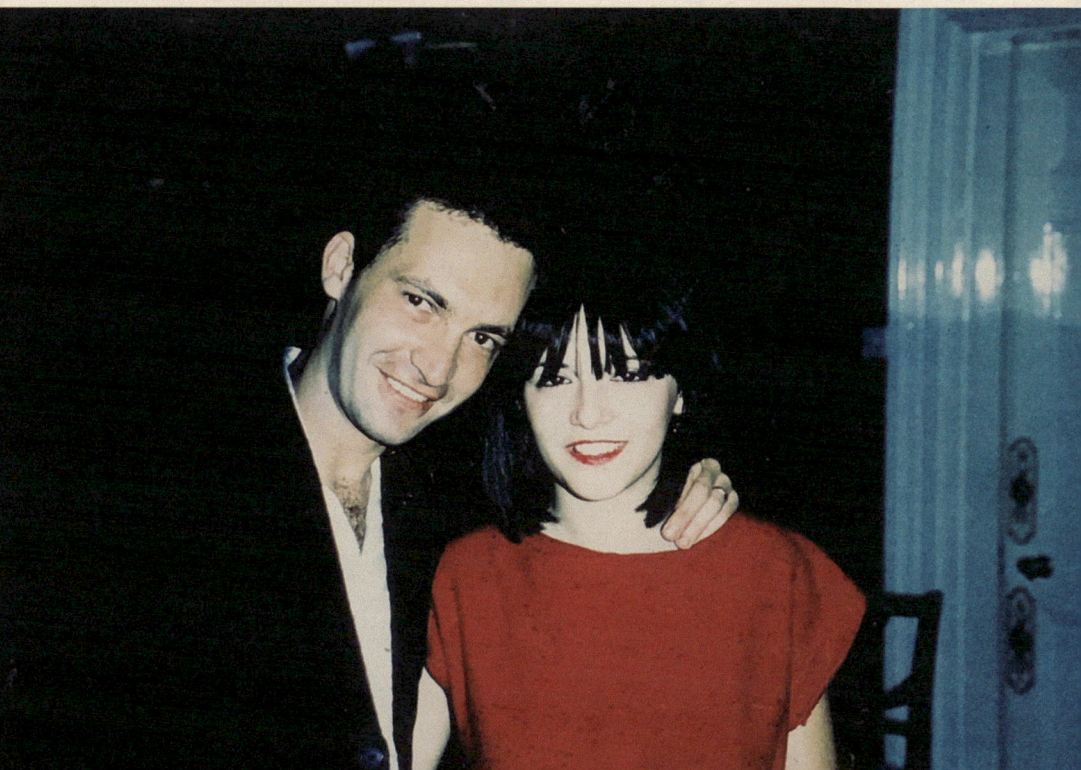

business. I would never wear jellies though because in the summer your feet would get hot and you'd slide in them.

The shop was pretty outrageous for the time and now—at this moment in time—it's quite hard to get that across because there might be lots of unusual looking places now.

Excuse me—I maintain even in today's cultural climate it would've stood out. There's nothing like that now.

No but I mean the way it looked. Since then, people have tried to replicate things like that but at that time there was absolutely nothing like that shop.

I'd maintain that still today—just because Top Shop is playing loud music it's not the fucking same. I actually can't think of a single place— I know there are shops that have a club vibe but when you walk in, it's a shop. Ours was not a shop, it was like walking into a club or somebody's home. There's no two ways about it. It was very individual, and I've never seen anything like it since.

It was to do with the changeover between two big cultural shifts. We saw a change in the way the people who shopped there looked.

Just before punk came in, it was the legacy of glam and the gay scene and the whole *Rocky Horror Picture Show* and Bowie boys. Then it started to be a bit more ripped, dishevelled, spiky, stripped down kinda vibe. Viv Albertine came in and we didn't know who she was. These people cut a striking form because there was really something going on here.

When we started at Acme, and I think for Jeannette as well as other white working-class kids in this country at the time—the big thing was Black music, specifically soul and reggae. They would never come into Acme and say, Don have you heard Pink Floyd? Have you heard ELO? No one was going to say that. So some of them set about creating music that reflected their situation—punk-rock. All of a sudden they're armed with a new soundtrack and that's when Jeannette took off— that's when she dumped me basically and became Jeannette Lee proper.

Instead of Jeannette Lee junior!

This white kid was involved in a culture that was ultimately alien because pre-punk there was a tradition of white working-class kids looking to Black music for their rebellious fix but now they had their own white version—it was an amazing thing to witness. That was a real trip.

One of the things that changed during that period and the shift from glam to punk was that in the beginning people like Rudolph Nureyev, Rod Stewart and Daryl Hall would come in to check out the shop and we were excited by that but then after about a year or so they were like the enemy. If people like them came in we would just take the piss and it would be like a joke that they were there because we had become 'punk' and this was the older generation that were all idiots and shouldn't be allowed to walk the earth. Don used to intimidate people.

Well, I would just wear dark glasses and not speak. I used to sit in the dentist chair—we had a dentist chair, which I loved and I just sat around looking cool. I wasn't unfriendly.

You were unfriendly. When someone famous came in, it quickly turned into... why would you come here? Iggy Pop was always around—I feel really ashamed of myself now—I spoke to Iggy a couple of times on the phone and he'd come round to Gunter Grove and knock on the door and we wouldn't let him in. Stuff like that. Even though he was great. But no one from the previous generation was allowed in.

When you start something new it's almost like Stalinist Revisionism where you've got to boot out the old. We all pretended that we didn't like the stuff we'd all grown up listening to. Ironically in the post-punk days many of us ended up buying back our Led Zeppelin records.

It was like shedding a skin. Shedding the old stuff.

Young people don't appreciate shades of grey—it's either this or that and I love that energy, personally. I think when you appreciate the 'greys' it kind of gets boring. That blind energy was a beautiful thing to be around. I count myself as really lucky to mix with these guys—her included—because it's all helped me to be who I am.

For whatever reason, John and Andrew decided they wanted

© Martin Brading

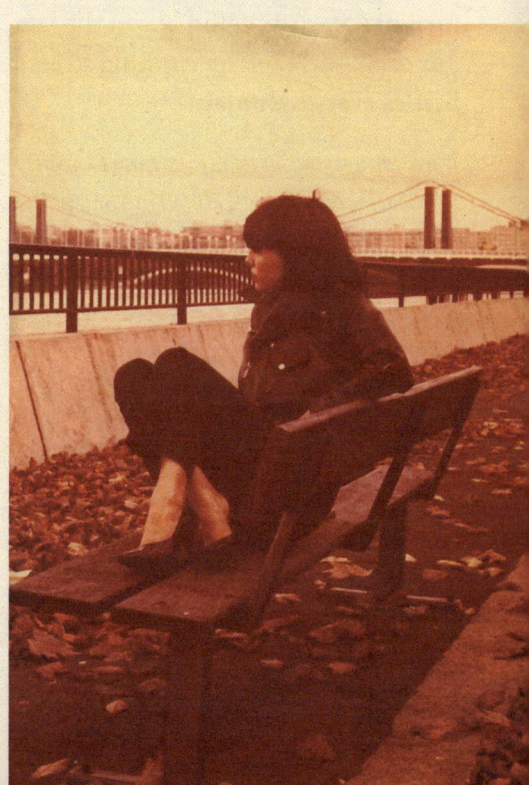

to change the look of the shop and they painted it black, which I hated. Basically they jumped on the tabloid bandwagon. All of a sudden they were getting things made that were copies of Vivienne and Malcolm that pandered to all that negative, almost swastikas, that stupid studs and leather vibe. Our lease ran out in the basement on Acme and they bought a shop on the Kings Road in Chelsea, which they named BOY. Jeannette and I opened that and by this time the whole tabloid punk thing had come to a head to the point of running street battles between punks and teddy boys. They were still around in the late 70s. Punk put the final nail in their coffin but in the late 70s there was literally running street battles every Saturday.

It was dangerous actually. Johnny Rotten got beaten up, he got stabbed by somebody. If you were walking down the wrong street and there was a bunch of teddy boys, you really were in trouble.

On Saturdays in BOY, which was glass-fronted—totally different to Acme Attractions—one minute you'd see 50 teds chasing a single punk down the road. Five minutes later you'd see 50 punks chasing a single ted down the road. It was literally that crazy. Sometimes it would actually spill into the shop—I remember having to lock people in and we'd have to fight people off from breaking the shop windows. It got really stupid. It turned into a shambles fairly quickly. I don't remember how long I was at BOY, do you?

No time.

BOY became a global phenomena— I left as I couldn't hold my head up in that place, it was an embarrassment. Do you remember the window display? Peter 'Sleazy' Christopherson who worked with Genesis P-Orridge did a window display of burnt body parts. Obviously fake.

They were all in boxes, like a severed arm or burnt ear, in the shop window for the opening of BOY.

Bit of controversy. So nurses see the window display, testify that the body parts are real and then the cops came and looked at them and realised they weren't but I got taken to court and was charged with indecent exhibition— apparently a law from the Napoleonic wars where you're not allowed to exhibit things like that for money or some shit—but yeah, that was the last straw for me so I left with the idea of 'trying' to manage the Slits—'trying' being the operative word.

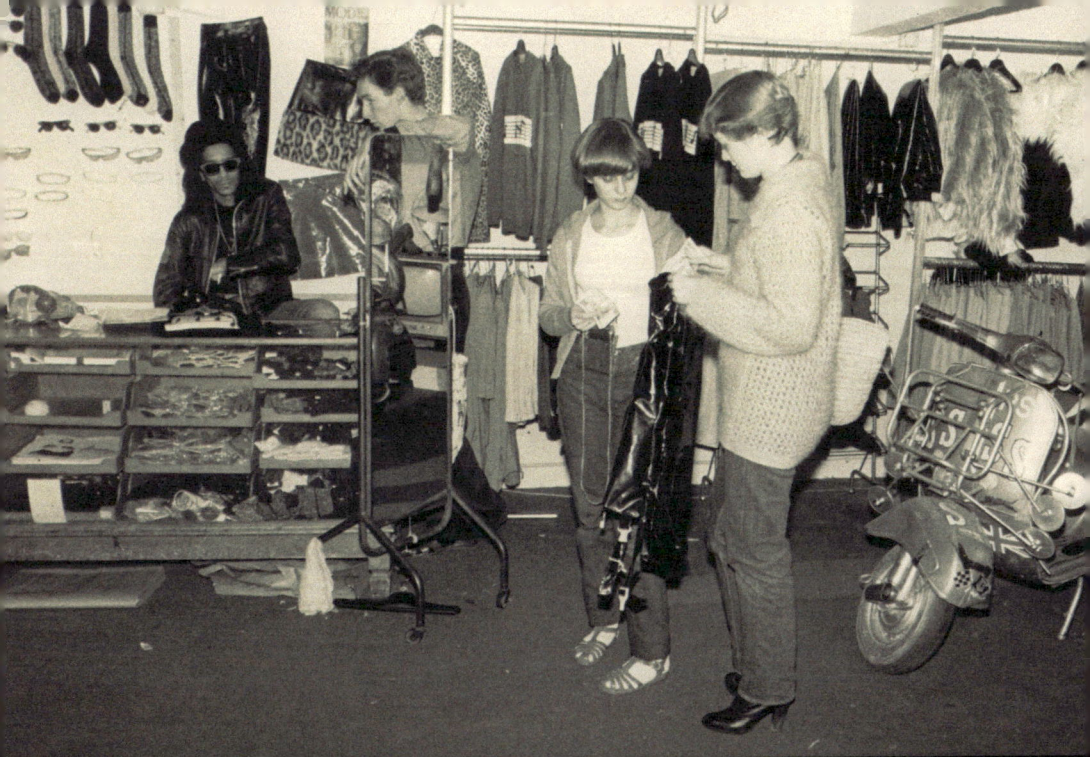

'BASICALLY, I TOOK MONEY FROM JOHN'S TILL, GAVE IT TO THE SLITS SO THEY COULD AFFORD TO GO ON THE WHITE RIOT TOUR WITH THE CLASH, BUZZCOCKS AND SUBWAY SECT—GREAT LINE UP'

Basically, I took money from John's till, gave it to the Slits so they could afford to go on the White Riot tour with the Clash, Buzzcocks and Subway Sect—great line up. But after that tour I realised that a) I didn't want to be a manager and b) they were unmanageable. The Slits were a trip man, on and off stage.

By this period, as a couple, we were on and off.

Yeah, she dumped me. It's good for the soul I think to be dumped—everyone needs to be dumped once. Not twice.

We accept that eventually don't we?

Yeah good for the soul. A tumultuous ending which stretched out a bit if I remember rightly but Jeannette then went off to join PIL.

I met John Lydon through Acme Attractions. As Don said there were two shops. There was SEX and there was Acme and all the cool kids went between the two. I don't think Vivienne liked John and Sid hanging out in Acme but they loved reggae and they smoked dope so they used to hang out in the shop. Don and Sid had a thing.

No, we didn't have a thing. He was a dick—I'm sorry.

No, he was quite sweet actually.

Yeah, a sweet dick—I was never sweet.

Anyway—so they used to hang out in the shop and that's how we got to know them so in a way that was the beginnings of my connection to PIL. PIL formed towards the end of Acme and the beginning of BOY and John Lydon or Rotten as he was known back then, asked me if I would join. I got to know John because he'd come to Forest Hill sometimes and hang out with us and then when the Sex Pistols split Don went to Jamaica with John. I was invited to go but I didn't have a passport and couldn't get one in time. I'm still smarting about that 'til this day.

That's right, John decided in Jamaica he was going to form PIL whilst we

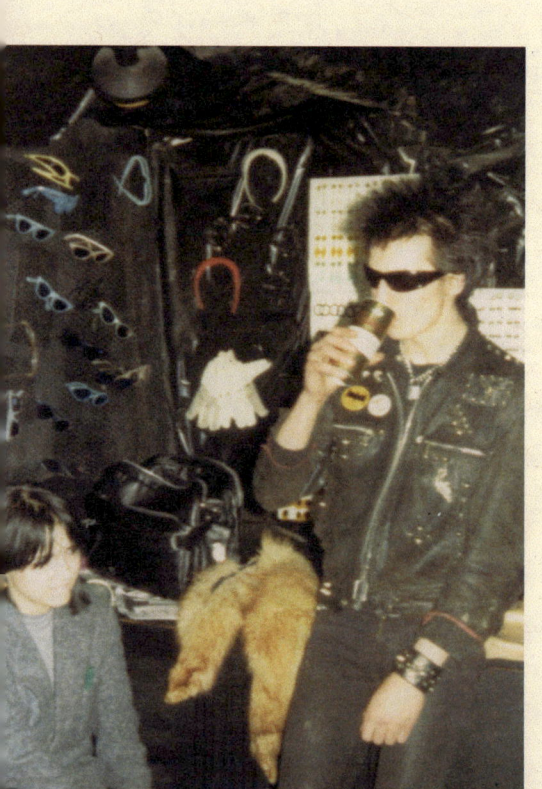

were there for two weeks. That was the most amazing trip of my life—first time to Jamaica and I was with Johnny Rotten and Richard Branson. He was starting a reggae label.

Acme was also the place where we met Joe Strummer and Mick Jones from the Clash too so it was the beginnings of Big Audio Dynamite for you. The actual meetings were in Acme. We didn't sit around in there thinking let's all form a group together but we all met in Acme.

Funnily enough Mick was the last one I got to know out of the Clash because he wasn't a big reggae head—he was the glam man. My first encounter with the Clash was Paul Simonon because he used to be a skinhead—the fashion version not the fascist version. If I could go back to any point in time it'd be the Acme days—best time of my life. The birth of punk-rock and who we are today.

It was a catalyst place where like-minded people were hanging out and talking about what they wanted to do next and all the key people in punk all came to Acme—we all met there.

Reggae was the glue—it was our mutual love.

I would also say that all of these people

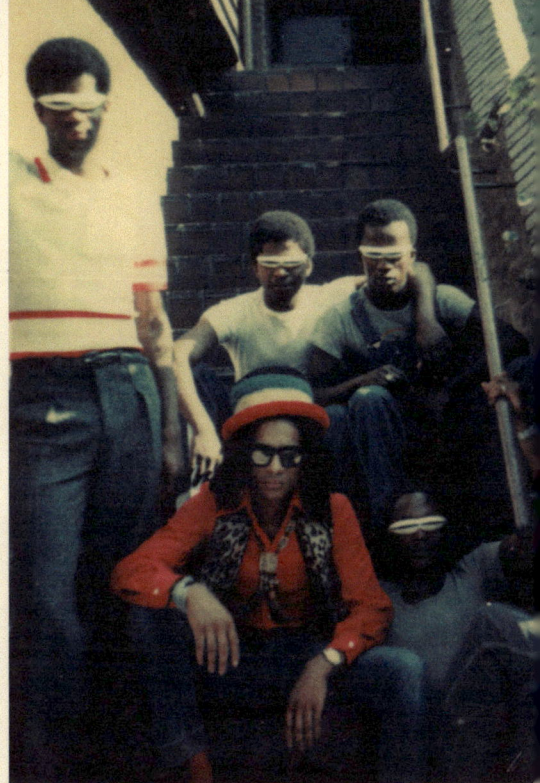

loved reggae but they didn't know any Black people at that point, that was a key factor.

Now funny we haven't said this, but the shop made a shitload of money, so much so we helped people out. The Slits would come in and if they were hungry we'd say, here you go, buy a meal. Chrissie would come in and say, I'm going to clean someone's house, we'd say, don't do that here's twenty quid. We were redistributing John and Steph's money. Nothing that would change their life but it might fill their bellies for that day.

A fiver was like £50 then. You used to earn £25 a week in the beginning and I earned £18 a week.

Yeah but it was abstract because our pockets were the tills so it meant nothing. What did you want for?

I'm not complaining Dad—I'm just saying.

If you did want something you probably wouldn't have to pay for it anyway because there was this weird black market thing going on where people from shops would trade with us. I remember getting a nice line of smoked salmon and caviar. My record collection was supplied by Harlequin—the record shop down the road.

There was a lot of trading going on in the Kings Road at that time so for instance the guy from HMV would come in after a reggae tape so he would swap twenty records for it. Then we had a thing going with the guy who ran SEX and we would exchange things—lots of that went on. It was like Deadwood. It was an amazing time. We had really open minds and open hearts to change and development. That's what it was.

We shared a common interest—I don't know how that happened—that we both happened to like things like Pink

'A LOT OF PEOPLE DON'T KNOW THIS BUT I WAS A BIG BEATLES FAN (STILL AM). I USED TO HAVE THE SECOND BIGGEST BEATLES MEMORABILIA COLLECTION IN THIS COUNTRY'

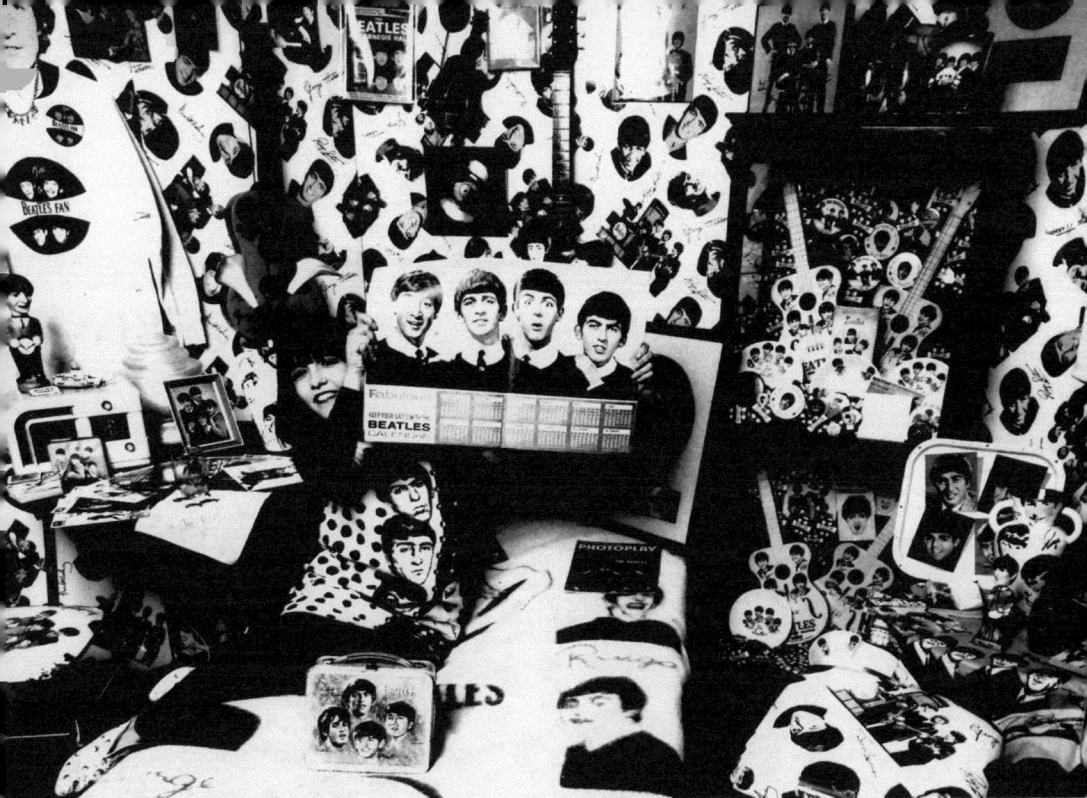

Flamingos, both of us had the same cultural references. Style-wise, art-wise. Our tastes were totally in sync, we were at that age where we were open and wanted to explore everything and take in as much information as possible—we were really open. I'd like to think we still are. I think in that youthful zest for life kinda way, I guess we bounced off each other to a certain degree. Late night films were a big deal in those days. We got an alternative education watching films.

It's like we're siblings and have grown up in the same family. We have the same reference points. Before the Roxy we would go to work all day on the Kings Road then we would go back to Forest Hill and play records and then we would go to a late night film at Paris Pullman, Notting Hill Gate or Scala—we would go and see things like El Topo—real sort of head films. We'd get back at 2.30am and open the shop at 10am the next morning. We were very active, doing stuff the whole time.

It wasn't a job though—I would've paid to do it, it was that much fun. I can't think of a single negative aspect. A lot of people don't know this but I was a big Beatles fan (still am). I used to have the second biggest Beatles memorabilia collection in this

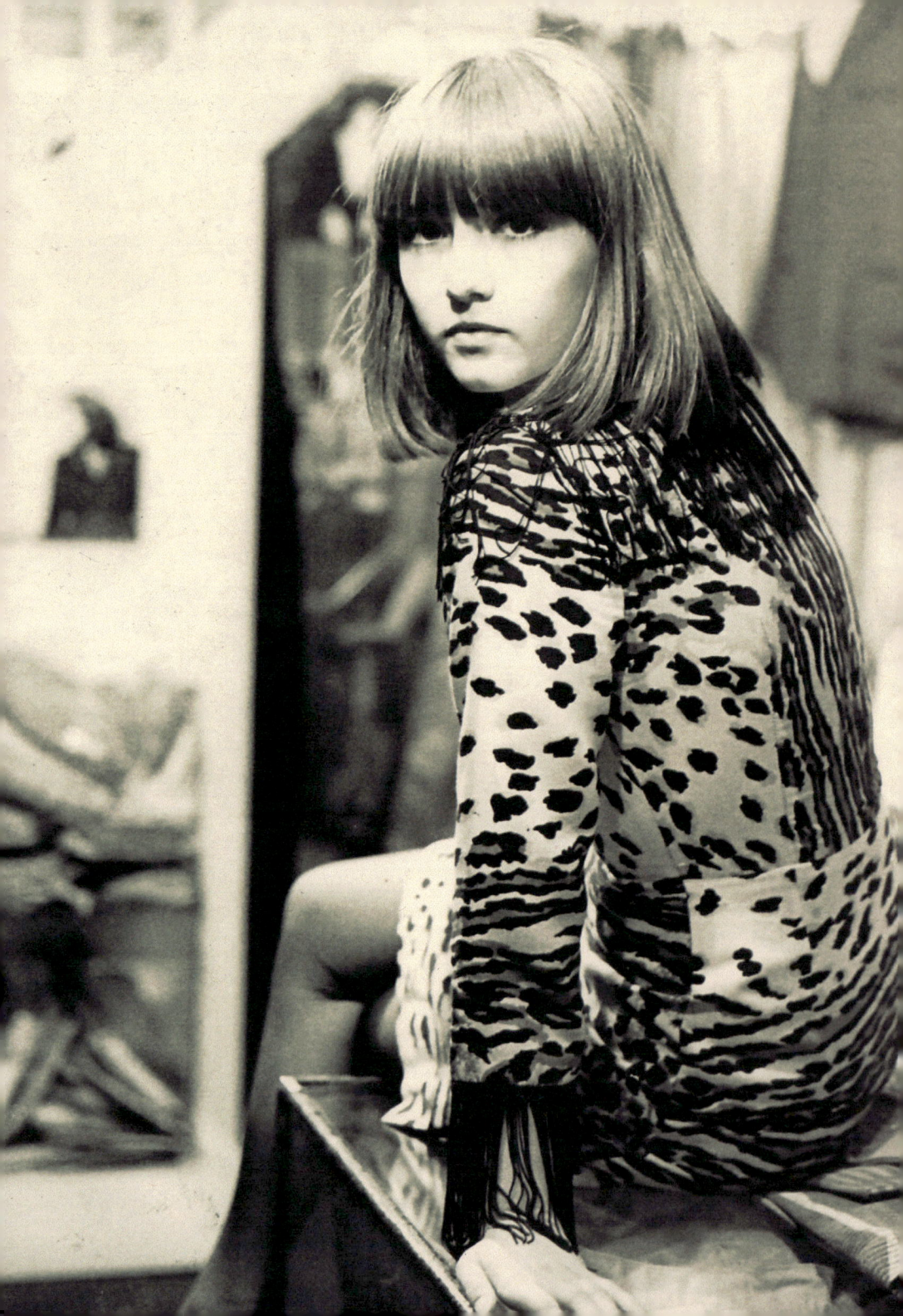

country. Steph Raynor also had a large Beatles collection and for whatever reason, we took this picture perhaps for a magazine to show our two collections. When punk came along, L'Uomo Vogue came to interview me about my Beatles collection and as I was doing the interview I had an epiphany of how ridiculous all this junk was. As a child of the vinyl generation the only thing that ever really mattered to me was the music. The next day I swapped it all with Steph, apart from the music, for a fuck off American car—like a *Starsky & Hutch* car only blue, not orange, with the big fuck off wheels at the back and that's why we kept getting pulled up. Then I think he sold it on and made a lot of money from it. Remember those pictures I stole from Apple, I gave one to Steph and you've got one on your wall now.

Yeah I got mine from a gallery though.

I was such a Beatle fan—I was what they called an 'Apple Scruff' who used to sit outside the studios on Saville Row. One day I blagged my way in with the security guard, I gave him twenty quid, went in and stole some negatives. Turned out that I couldn't have picked up a better bunch of negs. They were pictures taken by Astrid, Stuart Sutcliffe's girlfriend. It was like I'd picked up gold dust.

Weirdly a few years ago Geoff and I bought one of these images from a gallery for the Rough Trade Records office and I didn't realise it was from the same negatives.

I've still got the records but not any of the other stuff though and I don't regret it.

I still have that dress, though it wouldn't fit now.

Man you were pencil thin back then, must have been all the speed you were necking.

Excuse me! You're like one of those old men in a home who just come out and say anything, like someone out of Father Ted.

They are my heroes. I can't wait to get like that.

I think you're already there.

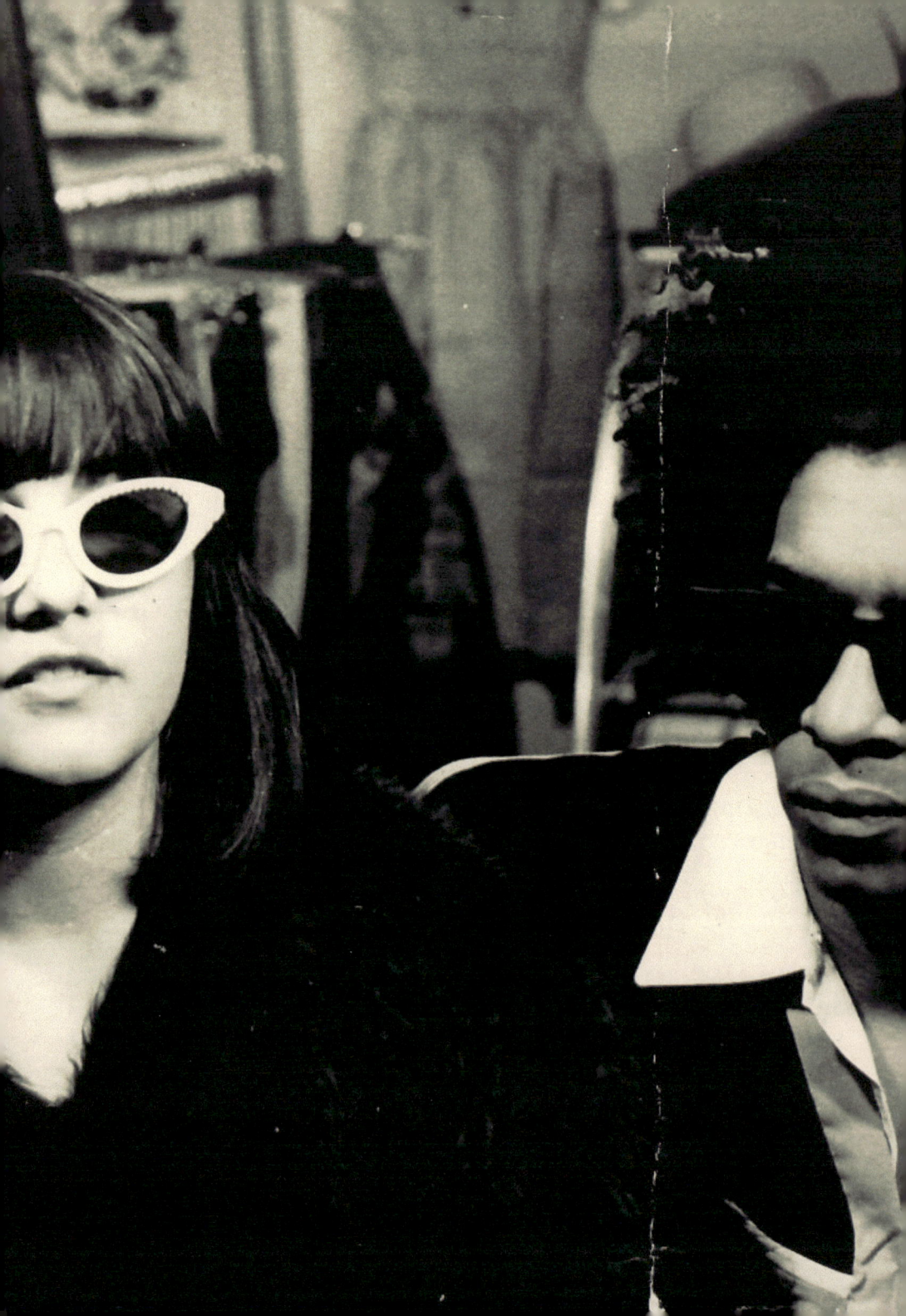